Cyhoeddwyd gan Rily Publications Ltd,
Blwch Post 257, Caerffili CF83 9FL
Hawlfraint yr addasiad © 2018 Rily Publications Ltd
Addasiad Cymraeg gan Bethan Mair

Cyhoeddwyd yn wreiddiol yn Saesneg yn 2015
dan y teitl *Happy Birthday to You!* gan Top That! Publishing Ltd.
© 2018 Tide Hill Media, wedi ei drwyddedu'n gyfyngedig i Top That Publishing Ltd

ISBN 978-1-84967-044-9

www.rily.co.uk

Tyrd i ganu
Pen-blwydd Hapus i Ti!

Pen-blwydd hapus i ti,
Pen-blwydd hapus i ti,

Mae'n ben-blwydd arna i!

Hwrê!

Pen-blwydd hapus, annwyl ⸻,
Pen-blwydd hapus i ti!

3

Pen-blwydd hapus, annwyl ⸻,
Dyma gardiau lond y tŷ!

I ti!

5

Pen-blwydd hapus, annwyl ....,
Dyma anrheg i ti!

7

Pen-blwydd hapus i ti,
Addurniadau fyny fry.

Pen-blwydd hapus, annwyl _____,
Addurniadau fyny fry!

9

Pen-blwydd hapus i ti,
Gwisgoedd ffansi – am sbri,

Sbarcleri yw fy hoff bethau!

Pen-blwydd hapus i ti,
Teisen befriog – waw wi,

Pen-blwydd hapus, annwyl _____,
Teisen befriog – waw wi!

Www!

Aaa!

FSSS!

13

Pen-blwydd hapus i ti,
Cwtshys pen-blwydd – un, dau, tri,

Pen-blwydd hapus!

Gwylia'r deisen!

Wps!

Ffrindiau gorau!

Pen-blwydd hapus, annwyl
Cwtshys pen-blwydd – un, dau, tri!

Pen-blwydd hapus i ti,
Hetiau lliwgar llawn sbri,

Pen-blwydd hapus, annwyl ....,
Hetiau lliwgar llawn sbri!

Pen-blwydd hapus i ti,
Popwyr parti, hi-hi!

18

POP!

Dwi'n sownd!

Pen-blwydd hapus, annwyl _____,
Popwyr parti, hi-hi!

19

Pen-blwydd hapus i ti,
Chwarae gemau nawn ni.

21

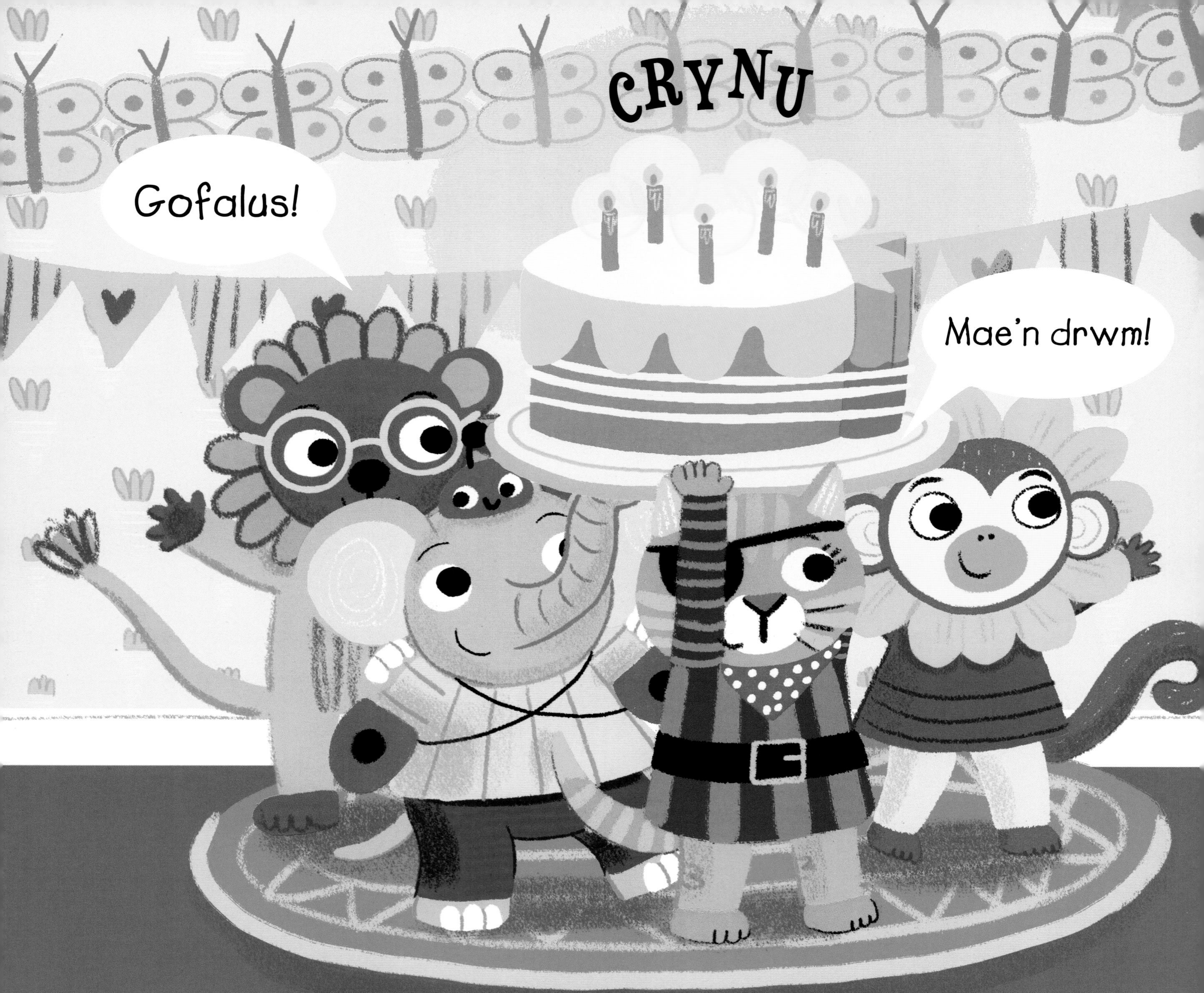

Pen-blwydd hapus i ti,
Teisen ben-blwydd i ti,

Mae'n anhygoel!

Pen-blwydd hapus, annwyl ....,
Teisen ben-blwydd i ti!

23

Pen-blwydd hapus i ti,
Gwna ddymuniad, da ti,
Pen-blwydd hapus, annwyl _____,
Gwna ddymuniad, da ti!

Gwna ddymuniad!

Sing-Along Happy Birthday to You!

2 Happy birthday to you,
Happy birthday to you,
Yippee! Yay!

It's my birthday!
Hooray!
Happy birthday, dear ... ... ,
Happy birthday to you!

4 Happy birthday to you.
These cards are for you,
From me with love.
To you from me.
I made it myself!

Happy birthday, dear . . . . . . ,
These cards are for you!
For you!

6 I hope you like it.
Thank you!
Happy birthday to you,
Birthday presents for you.

Happy birthday!
I chose it myself.
Can you guess what it is?
Happy birthday, dear . . . . . . ,
Birthday presents for you!

8 Pretty!
I love party flags!
Happy birthday to you,
Decorations for you,

We put them up ourselves!
Wow!
Happy birthday, dear . . . . . . ,
Decorations for you!

10 What are you?
I'm a lion!
Fancy dress is fun!
Happy birthday to you,
Fancy dress just for you.

I'm a butterfly!
Your costume is GREAT!
Happy birthday, dear . . . . . . ,
Fancy dress just for you!

12 Sparklers are my favourite.
Happy birthday to you,
Sparkly cupcakes for you.

Happy birthday, dear . . . . . . ,
Sparkly cupcakes for you!
Oooh! Aaah!
Fizzz!

14 Happy birthday to you,
Birthday hugs for you too,
Happy birthday!
Mind the cupcake!
Oops!
Friends are the best!

Happy birthday!
Happy birthday, dear . . . . ,
Birthday hugs for you too!

16 Now THAT'S a party hat!
Happy birthday to you,
Party hats pink and blue,

I love stripes!
I love spots!
Happy birthday, dear . . . . . . ,
Party hats pink and blue.

18 Ta-dah!
Happy birthday to you,
Party poppers, woo-HOO!

I'm in a tangle!
Happy birthday, dear . . . . . . ,
Party poppers, woo-HOO!

20 I hope I win!
Happy birthday to you,
Let's play games just for you,

What is it?
It's exciting!
Happy birthday, dear . . . . . . ,
Let's play games just for you!

22 Careful!
It's heavy!
Happy birthday to you,
Birthday cake made for you,

It's amazing!
Happy birthday, dear . . . . . . ,
Birthday cake made for you!

24 Happy birthday to you,
May your wishes come true,
Happy birthday, dear . . . . . . ,
May your wishes come true.

Make a wish!